THE MALVERN HILLS

Roger Redfern

First published in Great Britain in 2014

British Library Cataloguing-in-Publication Data
A CIP record for this title is available from the British Library

ISBN 978 0 85710 081 8

PiXZ Books
Halsgrove House, Ryelands Business Park,
Bagley Road, Wellington, Somerset TA21 9PZ
Tel: 01823 653777 Fax: 01823 216796
email: sales@halsgrove.com

An imprint of Halstar Ltd, part of the Halsgrove group of companies Information on all Halsgrove titles is available at: www.halsgrove.com

Printed and bound in China by
Toppan Leefung Printing Ltd

Contents

Roger Redfern

The late Roger Redfern, was once described as 'the doyen of countryside writers'. Much of his prolific and poetic writing about Britain's countryside, traditions and people appeared in over 700 entries for his regular Country Diary column in *the Guardian* newspaper spread over nearly 30 years.

He had walked extensively in all the hills and mountains of Britain since his childhood, and had an encyclopaedic knowledge of their landscapes, footpaths and hidden treasures away from the tourist 'honeypots'. Perhaps, his greatest love was exploring the high moorlands and dales of Derbyshire's Peak District, close to where he was born and brought up. It is said there isn't a summit from Cheshire to Lincolnshire on which he hadn't set foot.

His love of the British countryside is described in over 30 books covering England, Wales and Scotland, as well as hundreds of magazine articles. He spent every holiday away from his job as a teacher walking the 'high tops', a remote coastline or rolling countryside to experience their beauty and grandeur in all weathers and in all seasons.

The Malvern Hills were a particular favourite to which he returned time and time again. His teacher training in nearby Worcester meant he could follow in the footsteps and be inspired by the same scenery as his favourite composer, Sir Edward Elgar. He travelled the length of this shapely ridge for many decades until shortly before his death. Many of the walks in this book reflect his lifelong fascination with these hills; their ancient trackways, quiet woodlands and never-ending vistas.

Christopher Nicholson

How to use this book

The Area

The north – south hill range we call the Malvern Hills is unique in England, a sort of miniature mountain range of very ancient rocks that rises out of comparatively lowly territory on all sides. Seen from afar, especially from the north-west and the east, the hills look most impressive; distant views from the east reveal Great Malvern climbing the slopes of North Hill and Worcestershire Beacon like some hill town of northern India.

The Malverns are a designated Area of Outstanding Natural Beauty and are cared for by the Malvern Hills Conservators, a body established in 1884 for this very purpose.

The range extends about 8 miles (12.5 kms) from North Malvern southwards to Chase End Hill.

Routes and Maps

Each of the ten routes in this book are graded from Easy to More Challenging. With further details of distance, height ascended and the type of terrain covered, so assisting the reader to choose a suitable route. The information data contains details of distances and heights in both imperial and metric measures.

The walks described here require the following 1:25,000 Ordnance Survey maps to add interest and help avoid going astray:

Walks 1, 2, 5, 6, 7, 8, 9 and 10: Explorer Sheet 190. Walks 3 and 4: Explorer Sheet 204.

The maps in this book give only outlines to each route. Always go well equipped. If unsure of fitness try one of the easiest routes first! Not all of the routes described have convenient places providing refreshment so always take some food and drink.

Tell someone where you are going and your expected time of return. And, having checked the weather forecast, only tackle the longer routes in clear conditions.

Useful websites

Malvern Tourist Information Centre: www.malvern-hills.co.uk
Malvern Hills Conservators: www.malvernhills.org.uk
Elgar Birthplace Museum: www.elgarmuseum.org
Central Trains: www.centraltrains.co.uk
First Great Western: www.firstgreatwestern.co.uk

Key to Symbols Used

Level of difficulty:

Easy

Fair

More challenging

Map symbols:

Park & start

Walk route

Road/track

River/water

Building

Church

Pub

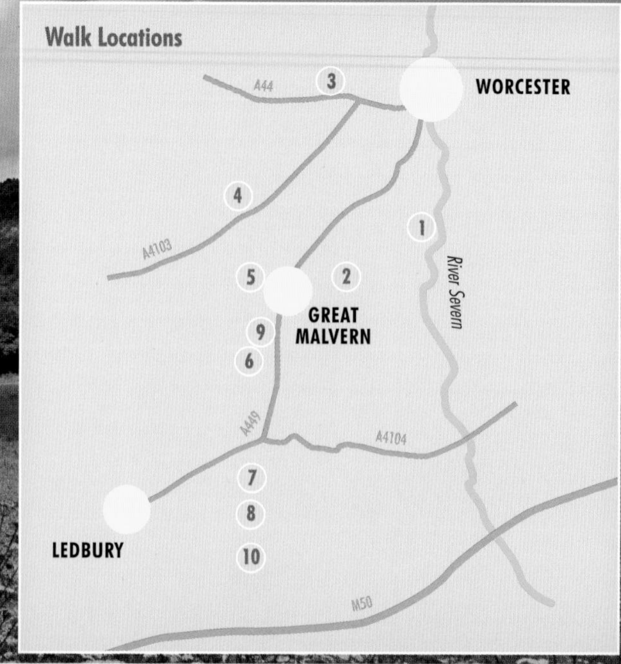

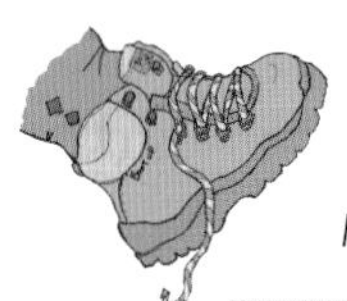

1 On the banks of the Severn

Far views of the Malvern Hills.

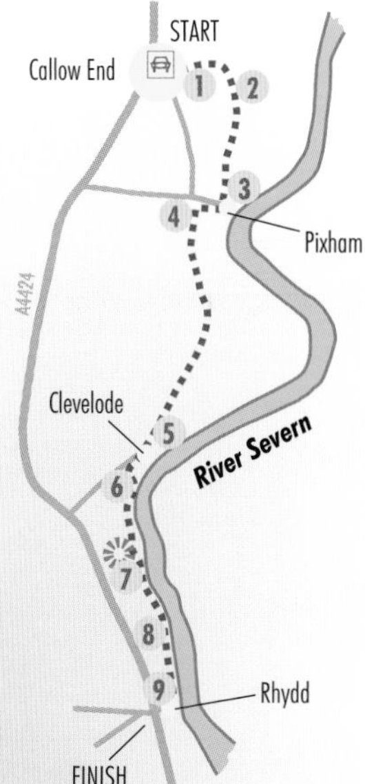

This linear walk down the western side of the River Severn is the most distant from the actual Malvern Hills of those described in this guide. It gives an introduction to the verdant Severn plain south of Worcester with good views most of the way to the hill range which is the centrepiece of the book.

Though summer is naturally a good time to walk here the abundant hedge and tree cover does preclude views of the nearby river in places. Gone are the days when this stretch of the river between Gloucester and Worcester was busy with commercial craft – carrying coal, clay, pottery, timber. These days the vessels plying here are pleasure craft and they add to the interest as we head south on foot between Callow End and Rhydd.

Level:
Length: 4 miles (6.5 kms).
Ascent: 230 feet (70 metres).
Terrain: Lanes, field and riverside paths.
Park and start: Callow End. GR837497.
Information: There is a request stop for bus service from Rhydd back to Callow End. Contact Great Malvern Tourist Information Centre. Tel. 01684 892289. Alternatively walk back to Callow End on the same riverside route.

Another vanished feature is the series of ferry crossings of the river all the way downstream of Worcester. On this route we see the site of Pixham Ferry, the one at Clevelode and finally at Rhydd where we leave the Severn's side. There are relics if you look for them – bits of jetties and the ferry-men's cottages.

The finest prospect of the eastern slopes of the Malvern Hills on this route is the 151 feet (46 metres) top of a conspicuous riverside hillock half a mile (.75 km) south of Clevelode village. Here is a copse of conifers, some long dead, that makes a dramatic foreground for the hills, four miles (6.5 kms) across Guarlford parish to the west.

1 Park at Callow End (near GR 837497).

2 Take the path that heads left (south-east) onto the flood plain and where two paths cross (beyond Moorhouse Farm) turn right (south) along the flood plain to the hamlet of Pixham.

3 Turn left to overlook the Severn and the site of the

Pixham House beside the River Severn.

The Malvern Hills from near Clevelode.

1 On the banks of the Severn

former Pixham Ferry near Pixham House.

4 Turn back to walk along Pixham Ferry Lane to the first road junction and here turn left along the level bridleway, keeping below Pixham Farm.

View north-east from top of river cliff near Clevelode.

The late Wilfrid Noyce, Himalayan mountaineer and teacher at Malvern College, once stated that no other hill range known to him resembled the Himalaya seen from afar as closely as the Malvern Hills.

Their sudden, abrupt rise from the Severn Plain on the east and the crumpled Herefordshire countryside to the west is certainly unique in the British Isles. Composed of ancient Pre-Cambrian rock that rises to 1,395 feet (425 metres) at Worcestershire Beacon directly above Great Malvern town, this upthrust or highland backbone has resisted the effects of weathering extremely well through the past five hundred million years. From the crest of this miniature mountain range you can see fourteen counties in clear weather. Little wonder that several tops were chosen in pre-history to site fortifications.

5 Beyond Frieze Wood go over the levee (anti-flood bank) and climb to higher ground to reach the tree-girt, riverside hamlet of Clevelode on this bridleway.

6 Come down a drive at Clevelode and turn right along the public lane for a few metres then take the footpath signposted to the left. This soon runs close to the river

The old ferry landing on the Severn at Rhydd.

but hidden from it by the steep and scrubby woodland that clings to the river cliff.

7 In due course a short climb brings us to the group of conifers with that fine view to the Malvern Hills mentioned in the introduction.

8 The path soon descends to the riverside and we are soon at the site of the former Rhydd Ferry.

9 Turn right up the lane to the main road at Rhydd (junction of B4211 and B4424).

Cabin cruiser on the Severn at Rhydd.

Houseboat on the Severn passing Rhydd.

2 A great medieval park

On foot at Madresfield.

Between Malvern Link and the River Severn the magnificent Madresfield Park surrounds Madresfield Court, ancestral home of the Lygon family since 1260.

They were raised to the Earldom of Beauchamp in 1815 and Madresfield is probably best remembered as the model for Evelyn Waugh's "Brideshead".

Here is a medieval park still with an impressive avenue of trees along the eastern approach to the house. Throughout the park, too, are ancient oaks and pockets of well managed woodland.

Our walking route starts and ends in the estate village of Madresfield, dominated by the parish church of St Mary the Virgin. Edward Elgar was fortunate that the Lygon family were the first aristocrats to show a serious interest in his music. Indeed, Lady Mary Lygon, sister of Earl Beauchamp ran a local music festival at Madresfield Court and Elgar became closely involved with it in the early

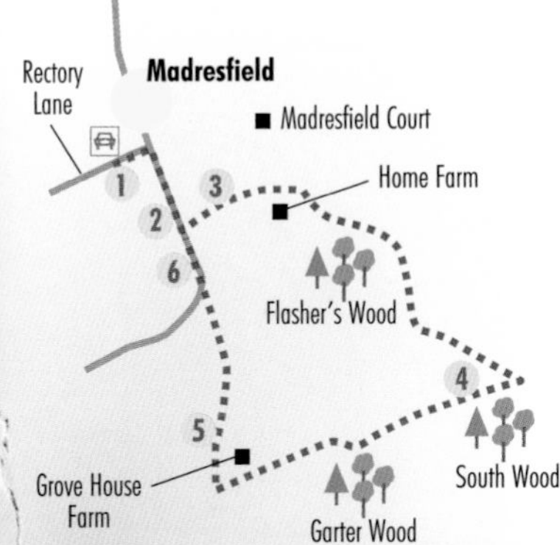

Level:
Length: 3.75 miles (6 kms).
Ascent: Negligible.
Terrain: Level drive, field paths and public road.
Park and Start: Rectory Lane, Madresfield. GR 803474.
Information: Refreshments in Great Malvern.

years of the twentieth century. By 1913 he was so well considered that Earl Beauchamp invited him to stay as a guest at Madresfield Court.

We are not allowed to go close to the great house but there are clear glimpses of it as we head towards the Home Farm. We skirt several small woods and the meandering Whiteacres Brook on its sinuous travels to the Severn.

Out on the plain we are able to look back westwards to see Great Malvern spreading up the steep flanks of North Hill and Worcestershire Beacon – like some Indian hill town or Mediterranean coastal resort.

Church Cottage, Madresfield.

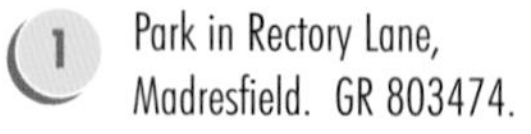

1 Park in Rectory Lane, Madresfield. GR 803474.

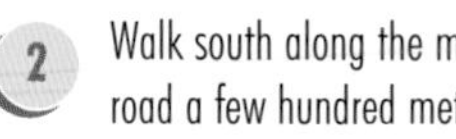

2 Walk south along the main road a few hundred metres.

3 Turn left at the lodge to Madresfield Court and proceed east along the drive and immediately past the Home Farm (on the right) turn on the path heading south-east round the northern edge of Flasher's Wood and pass through smaller Bills

Madresfield Court from the Park.

Wood to reach the northern edge of South Wood.

Ancient oak in Madresfield Park.

In his book England's Thousand Best Houses (Penguin/Alan Lane, 2003) Simon Jenkins considers Madresfield Court one of the "Top Hundred". This is not surprising considering the history and architecture involved here in the shadow of the Malvern Hills.

Home of the Lygons for seven centuries this is a house of many styles; medieval much modified and added to when the architect Philip Hardwick set to work in 1865 on the instructions of the sixth Earl Beauchamp and his son, the seventh Earl who later fell foul of the "Establishment" with scandalous "goings on".

It is a place crammed with fabulous possessions and though there has never been a contents sale here – unlike so many other English stately homes – Lady Morrison, niece of the last Earl, did hold what came to be called a "Rolls Royce Boot Sale" here in the park in 1996 when she raised cash for charity.

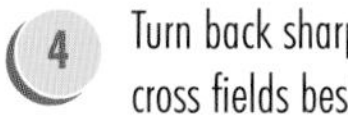

Turn back sharply right to cross fields beside Garter Wood.

St Mary the Virgin church from Madresfield Park.

5 Follow the path round Grove House Farm to head north through fields to re-join the public road.

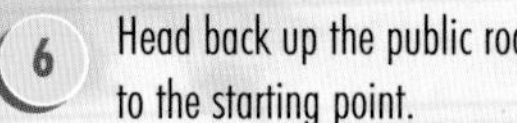

6 Head back up the public road to the starting point.

The Malvern Hills from Madresfield Park.

North Hill from Madresfield Park.

3 Heart of Elgar country

On foot where it all began.

The Malvern Hills are synonymous with Edward Elgar, considered by many this country's greatest composer. This route takes us across the fields to his birthplace at Lower Broadheath, three miles (4.75 kms) west of Worcester, and close by Broadheath Common where as a tiny tot he must have been taken and in maturity he wandered here with his dogs, fondly remembering early, carefree days. His "Wand of Youth" suites were an evocation of those Broadheath days.

Lower Broadheath
Laylocks Garden Centre
Elgar's Birthplace
A44
Atchen Hill
Cotheridge
Otherton Lane
A4103
Howsen Farm
River Teme
Bransford Bridge
1 2 3 4 5 6 7 8 9 10 11 12

We turn our backs on Broadheath to head towards Cotheridge village with its remarkable Norman church and eventually come down to the left bank of the Teme and return to our starting point at Bransford Bridge over the river. In the main we cover gently undulating lowland farmland, often with fine vistas south-west towards the Malvern Hills, about five miles (8 kms) away.

Level: ♥ ♥
Length: 6.25 miles (10 kms).
Ascent: 130 feet (40 metres).
Terrain: Field paths and public roads.
Park and Start: Bransford Bridge. GR 804533.
Information: At Elgar Centre. GR 806558. Refreshments at Fox Inn, Bransford Bridge and at Laylocks Garden Centre. GR 801541.

1 Park and start at the Fox Inn beside Bransford Bridge over the River Teme. GR 804533.

2 Cross the bridge and immediately go left on the footpath beside the Teme's north bank.

The River Teme from Bransford Bridge.

3 Cross the tributary stream on a rickety footbridge where it drains down into the Teme. Turn right (north) and aim for a stile at the far end of the pasture; skirt round the eastern edge of the next field, cross a stile then head north-west to reach Howsen Farm.

Caractacus and Sir Edward Elgar may be the first two names that come to mind in connection with the Malvern Hills but it is the latter we are concerned with here.

One of the highlights of the route described here is Sir Edward's birthplace at Lower Broadheath. Born here in June, 1857 he spent the first two years of his life here before the family moved to Worcester but he and his siblings often spent holidays at a nearby farm.

He had great affection for the Malvern Hills that rise in full view across the plain to the south and in later life he lived at various locations upon the Malvern's slopes. Upon the Malvern Hills, too, he cycled, flew kites, motored and walked his dogs. It is true to say that much of his music was conceived within sight of the hills, has the spirit of the place about it.

In old age he returned to his beloved Worcestershire and his homes at Kempsey and Rainbow Hill, Worcester had good views across the Severn to that favourite profile of this "miniature mountain range".

The Malvern Hills from Otherton Lane.

4 Turn left on gaining the bridleway to cross the farmyard. At the side of the brick building on the right turn right up the field.

5 Skirt the right-hand edge of the next field and go down to cross the gloomy dingle and so along the grassy drive to the A44 road. Here, on the left, is Laylocks Garden Centre (refreshments).

6 Walk right (east) along the A44 to the junction with Otherton Lane (on the right) and now look behind a thicket opposite Otherton Lane-end for the continuation of the Three Choirs Way and follow this uphill to the road on Atchen Hill.

Elgar's Birthplace, Lower Broadheath.

Elgar's summerhouse at the Birthplace, removed from Marl Bank, Worcester – the composer's last home.

7 Turn left along the road to locate Elgar's Birthplace and the Elgar Centre (on the right behind The Plough Inn).

8 On leaving this Elgar "shrine" turn right and walk to the first cross-roads.

St Leonard's church at Cotheridge is mainly Norman and has what is reputed to be the oldest extant timber tower in Worcestershire. It was erected in the fifteenth century using two overlapping crucks and lots of braces to counteract the swinging of the bells. By 1961 it was decided the bell frame could no longer safely support the four bells so three were sold for scrap and the fourth retained. A more dramatic event occurred fourteen years earlier when the nave roof collapsed, resulting in comprehensive re-building and internal modifications.

9 Turn left along the lane all the way to its junction with the A44 road. Take the footpath directly opposite that curves behind a bungalow and continues to Cotheridge's ancient church of St Leonard.

St. Leonard's Church, Cotheridge.

Resting flock at Lower Court, Cotheridge.

10 Walk left (south) down the lane to its end at Lower Court Farm with its giant Wellingtonia tree, a remnant of the former Berkeley estate.

11 Go down the path that starts opposite the lane-end and this very gently descends, swinging round to the left to reach the rickety footbridge we crossed early on this route.

12 Keep on the footpath close above the left (north) bank of the Teme to return to Bransford Bridge.

4 Storridge and the Suckley Hills

Exploring more of Elgar's own country.

Whereas the first three routes in this guide cross generally level lowland adjacent to the Severn and Teme this one is over steeper, hillier terrain. It lies in that crumpled country that is something of a northward extension of the Malvern Hills, though attaining only more modest altitudes.

This crumpled ground is still much wooded and includes Bearswood Common, The Beck and the Suckley Hills. The district has long been famous for its fruit trees and those in the know come here each spring to see the brilliant blossom in the damson and other orchards.

This district attracted Edward Elgar in his mature years, such a contrast to the hustle and bustle of the city life associated with his music making.

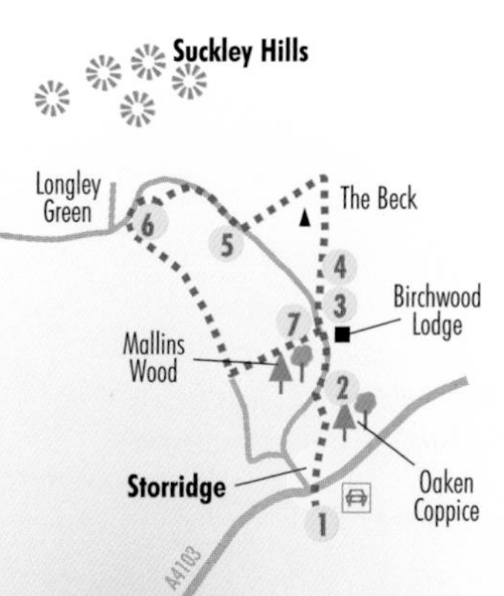

Level:
Length: 4.5 miles (7.25 kms).
Ascent: 470 feet (143 metres).
Terrain: Public lanes, fields and woodland paths.
Park and Start: Storridge village. GR 752485.
Information: Refreshments at inn about 1.25 miles (2 kms) along A4103 towards Worcester. Also at inn about 1.5 miles (2.5 kms) westwards along A4103 at Stafford's Bridge.

There are places near Storridge and Longley Green where you can see the western slopes of North Hill (1302 feet/ 397 metres) rising above nearby wood slopes and you could easily imagine yourself close to Betws-y-Coed in Snowdonia. This northern end of the Malvern Hills really does take on the countenance of mountains, transporting the observer's mind into remoter territory.

Birchwood Lodge.

View west over Leigh Brook Valley to Grove Hill.

1 Park in Storridge village, near the junction of the B4219 with the A4103. GR 752485.

2 Cross the A4103 to the north side and take the path heading up into Oaken Coppice.

Birchwood Lodge, Storridge stands near the 670 feet (204 metres) summit of The Beck above the valley containing Storridge village. At the end of the nineteenth century it must have seemed more isolated from the world than now and that is what so attracted Edward Elgar to the place.

In 1898 he was able to start renting it from the local squire as a retreat while living at Great Malvern and, from 1899, Malvern Wells. The composer loved Birchwood Lodge and if it had been possible would have bought the place. It was here that he worked on "Caractacus" and "Sea Pictures" and completed one of his greatest works, "The Dream of Gerontius" in the summer of 1900.

A countryman at heart he was able during his stays here to indulge in all manner of activities from felling trees and kite flying to cycling and fox hunting. Alas, in 1903 he had to hand in the lease on Birchwood Lodge and this was a real blow. Writing to a friend he complained about "giving up of little things which I love". Throughout the rest of his life he kept returning to this district where he had been so happy for five years of his middle age.

Today Birchwood Lodge is readily recognizable complete with a plaque above the front door celebrating those happy, creative years 1898 – 1903. But the house has been enlarged to side and rear, though the broad vista eastwards towards Worcester remains.

Once through the trees you gain the public lane that leads to Birchwood and Longley Green. Turn right and follow the lane.

3 At Birchwood Farm look right along the drive and see Birchwood Lodge, once a retreat for Sir Edward Elgar.

Winthill above the Cradley Brook.

Oast houses above Suckley.

4 Continue along the lane a further few hundred yards then take the footpath forking ahead to the right. We skirt along the east side of the 670 feet (204 metres) summit of The Beck before turning left along a path back to the lane.

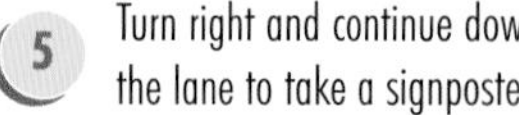

5 Turn right and continue down the lane to take a signposted

The western slopes of the Malvern Hills from above Cradley Brook.

path to the left which gives access to a lovely, green valley with prospects of quiet woods.

6 On joining the same lane lower down turn left along it a very short distance before taking the next path on the left to head for almost a mile (1.5 km) then take a path (left) that heads up through Mallins Wood to re-join the lane a short distance south of the drive to Birchwood Lodge.

7 Turn right (south) along the lane then take the path (left) down through Oaken Coppice back to the starting point at Storridge.

Bearswood Common from the valley of the Cradley Brook.

5 To Worcestershire Beacon

Setting foot on the highest Malvern hill.

At 1,394 feet (425 metres) the Worcestershire Beacon is the highest of the Malvern Hills. It stands about half a mile (.75 km) south-west of Great Malvern's town centre and about 900 feet (275 metres) above it.

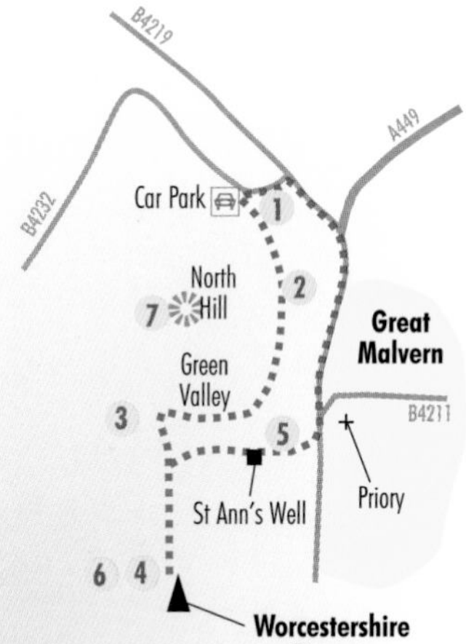

Ever since the district became popular with affluent visitors – mainly on account of the reputation of its health-giving spring waters – from the late eighteenth century the summit of Worcestershire Beacon has been a goal for the more intrepid visitors, largely on account of its fabulous 360 degrees view. Those unable or unwilling to go on foot were, at one time, conveyed there by donkey, even in bath chairs!

Level: ✿ ✿
Length: 2.5 miles (4 kms) ending in central Great Malvern or 3 miles (5 kms) if returning to the starting point.
Ascent: 820 feet (250 metres) without traversing the top of North Hill.
Terrain: Hillside paths with steep uphill and downhill slopes.
Park and start: Car park (pay and display) above North Malvern Road. GR 770470.
Information: Information at Great Malvern Tourist Information Centre. Tel. 01684 892289. Refreshments in Great Malvern and St Ann's Well.

The most direct (and steepest) route from Great Malvern climbs straight up behind the Priory to pass St Ann's Well; but a more devious and interesting way is described here, going round the eastern flank of neighbouring North Hill and so approaching the highest top from that northern side.

There used to be a wooden cabin on the actual top of Worcestershire Beacon, a shelter and source of refreshments, but this was destroyed by fire and the site completely cleared so that its exact location is difficult to judge.

The Malvern Hills from Priory Park, Great Malvern.

The Clock Tower, North Malvern.

1 Start at the "pay and display" car park above North Malvern Road. GR 770470.

2 Walk up the woodland path that ascends slantwise up the eastern flank of North Hill.

3 Go steeply up to the right, climbing through Green Valley to gain the open col between North Hill and Worcestershire Beacon.

4 Turn left and tackle the northern slopes of

Looking west from near the summit of Worcestershire Beacon.

Great Malvern from the northern slopes of Worcestershire Beacon.

Worcestershire Beacon – there are several alternative paths – to gain the open summit with its trig. pillar and annotated viewer.

5 The quick, direct way down from the summit is to descend to Green Valley and continue straight down to St Ann's Well and proceed down good paths to gain Great Malvern directly above the Priory.

Evening on Worcestershire Beacon looking across the Severn Valley.

St Ann's Well is situated on the eastern slopes of Worcestershire Beacon, directly above the centre of Great Malvern. There are many springs issuing from the ancient rock strata of the Malverns, each one claiming miraculous health-giving properties. St Ann's Well is the best known and seen by the most people, the majority on the way to the top of Worcestershire Beacon. A pretty, ornate cottage adjoins the well and serves as a useful café.

One of the most interesting of Malvern's water springs is situated on the northern slope of North Hill, adjacent to North Malvern Road. The tank or reservoir here was originally one of the largest in all the Malvern Hills, providing all North Malvern's water requirements from 1835.

In 1843 the tower we see today was built on top of the tank, complete with a clock for the benefit of the local population. Sadly it never kept accurate time – probably due to the vibrations caused by blasting in the nearby stone quarries !

6 Alternatively, simply retrace your steps all the way to the starting point at the car park.

7 A second alternative would be to return from the col at the head of Green Valley by traversing the summit of North Hill then descend eastwards for an eventual traverse north to the starting point car park.

North Hill from Worcestershire Beacon.

6 A circuit near Evendine

On the western slopes above Colwall.

Jubilee Drive is the delightful, level B4232 road that contours along the western flank of the central part of the Malvern Hills – below Perseverance Hill, Jubilee Hill, Pinnacle Hill and Black Hill – between the Wyche Cutting and Wynds Point on the A449.

Much of it passes through the tilting woods that cover this mid-height, western side of the range. Here and there we reach a clearing that reveals glimpses of the gorgeous, rolling terrain of eastern Herefordshire as far as the blue profiles of the Welsh borderland and beyond.

Level:
Length: 2.75 miles (4.5 kms).
Ascent: 330 feet (100 metres).
Terrain: Field and woodland paths. Some steep slopes.
Park and start: Gardiner's Quarry car park. GR 766421.
Information: Refreshments at "The Kettle Sings" restaurant near the starting point.

This suggested route starts near the conveniently situated "The Kettle Sings" restaurant just below Gardiner's Quarry car park and we do an anticlockwise circuit as we descend through woodland, parkland and pasture land to reach the scattered settlement of Evendine before a steady climb through quiet woodland and silent fields with, here and there, grand views back to the northern face of the Herefordshire Beacon and its complex, prehistoric earthworks.

1 Park at Gardiner's Quarry car park (pay and display). GR 766421.

The unique "The Kettle Sings" restaurant was established here, just below Jubilee Drive, on the western slope of the Malvern Hills in 1928. It must have probably the finest views looking westwards across Herefordshire of any such establishment in all of England.

Good use is made of the vista from its windows and patio because annotated photographs are available on the tables which explain highlights visible in clear weather. We learn that the Brecon Beacons lie 50 miles (80 kms) away; Hay Bluff in the Black Mountains and the conspicuous Sugar Loaf are 33 miles (53 kms) distant; Radnor Forest is 40 miles (64 kms) away; and the various Colwall villages stand on the sloping foothills just below our belvedere.

Looking west over Herefordshire to the Welsh mountains from "The Kettle Sings".

2 Walk down the narrow lane that forks north-west (left) off Jubilee Drive opposite the car park.

3 In about 400 yards (400 metres) look for a footpath on the left between tall trees. Go down this often wet and muddy path to reach a drive.

4 Turn left along the drive and keep right where the

Worcestershire Beacon from above Colwall.

Herefordshire Beacon from the path to Evendine.

Herefordshire Beacon from below Jubilee Drive.

The spring water issuing from various springs in the Malvern Hills has been renowned for centuries and the spring at Colwall, here on the western side of the main watershed, has seen its supply bottled commercially by Schweppes since 1850. Latterly purchased by Coca-Cola the bottling plant was finally closed in the autumn of 2010 because, it was claimed, it was too small to be profitable. This was largely due to the amount of water it was possible to extract each day so that it could not compete on price.

Near Evendine.

drive enters the grounds of Linden House.

5 Continue below the mansion to a gate.

6 Cross the stile at the gate and turn right down a path (this is the Geopark Way) through the field and near a barn (on the right) turn left

and keep slightly uphill to enter a hill-side plantation before traversing the edges of several fields with the profile of the Herefordshire Beacon ahead.

7 Continue ahead along the broad track all the way to the public lane at Evendine.

8 Turn left up the lane and where it curves to the right walk up the drive ahead to reach the semi-bungalow called "Spindrift" and go behind it to follow the path right up through the wood.

9 Enter two wood-encircled fields and then enter another wood and keep straight up the path, ignoring paths branching left and right.

A last glimpse of Herefordshire from Jubilee Drive

Soon enter "the Kettle Sings" car park and return to Gardiner's Quarry car park.

7 Over Herefordshire Beacon to Pink Cottage

A circuit over a major prehistoric earthwork.

The lofty hill range of the Malverns was an attraction for local tribes in prehistory. The summits offered good vantage points and ideal sites for defence in troubled times. By far the most important and impressive is the remains of the so-called British Camp upon the 1,109 feet (338 metres) top of the Herefordshire Beacon, south of the col we know as Wynd's Point and from where this route begins.

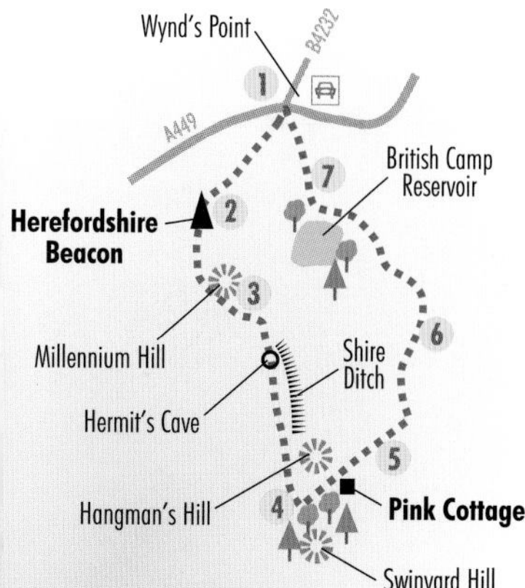

The way now lies southwards from the summit, passing the famous Hermit's Cave (often called Clutter's Cave) cut out of the ancient rock at some date unknown. Running right along the north – south watershed is the so-called Shire Ditch and it takes us over the next top – Hangman's Hill – then we are descending towards Swinyard Hill.

Level:
Length: 2.5 miles (4 kms).
Ascent: 650 feet (200 metres).
Terrain: Ridge-top paths and woodland tracks. Some steep inclines.
Park and start: Car park (pay and display) at Wynd's Point. GR 764404.
Information: Refreshments at snack bar and hotel at Wynd's Point.

A path turns back eastwards and we skirt the rear of Pink Cottage before entering a tilting wood and so eventually we swing back northwards to climb steeply past the delightfully sited British Camp Reservoir and the access road to this waterworks soon brings us to our starting point on the col called Wynd's Point.

This circular route has the advantage of passing through contrasting landscapes in fairly rapid succession – open hilltop and ridge, steep descent, woodland traverse and reservoir-side. Very satisfying.

Ramparts of the British Camp on Herefordshire Beacon.

1 Start at the car park (pay and display) at Wynd's Point. GR 764404.

Climb the broad path to the top of Herefordshire Beacon, noticing the complex system of ditches forming the British Camp.

3 Continue south along the crest of the ridge, over Millennium Hill to reach the col at GR 762395.

View northwards over Colwall to the Clee Hills from Herefordshire Beacon.

Upon the summit slopes of the Herefordshire Beacon, at about the mid point of the Malvern Hills watershed, lies the British Camp. This is a remarkable remnant from the Iron Age covering 44 acres, its central citadel being a stone wall 50 yards in circumference and 60 feet above the fosse or ditch. The Normans are said to have re-used the citadel because of its advantageous situation. It is also thought to have been used by the Welsh leader Owain Glyndwr in 1405 to rally his troops against the English. Probably the finest prehistoric fortification remaining in this country.

Hermit's Cave south of Millennium Hill.

Follow the directions on the stone indicator to pass the Hermit's Cave then continue along beside the Shire Ditch to reach Hangman's Hill. There's a good view south-west to the obelisk above Eastnor Castle, an object of interest on the next route.

Looking to Worcestershire Beacon from Herefordshire Beacon.

British Camp Reservoir and the Cotswolds from Millennium Hill.

The Shire Ditch that runs almost the entire length of the Malvern Hills watershed is believed to have been constructed about 1287 by Gilbert de Clare to form a physical boundary between his lands and those of the Bishop of Hereford over on the western side.

4 At the low point ahead, before the rise to Swinyard Hill, turn back (left) along the track to pass behind Pink Cottage.

5 Enter the woods beyond Pink Cottage and descend quite steeply towards Shadybank Common.

6 Follow the track that now heads due north to enter the deep woods clothing Tinker's Hill then climb the steep track to eventually come level with the surface of British Camp Reservoir (on left).

7 Follow the drive that ascends through the woods to enter the car park at Wynd's Point.

Foxgloves below Hangman's Hill.

8 Berrow Downs, the Obelisk and Shadybank Common

On the trail to a great monument.

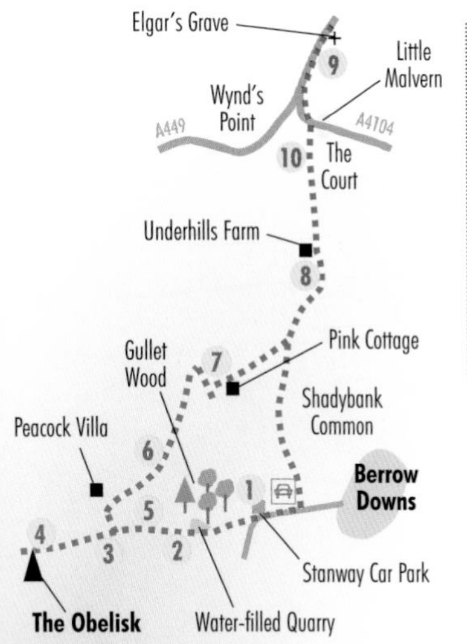

This route, unlike the others in this guide, tends to run east to west, then west to east crossing the watershed of the Malvern Hills from the low lying Berrow Downs to reach the ridge-top where stands the great obelisk commemorating Lord Somers with views down towards Eastnor Castle in the crumpled territory of eastern Herefordshire.

A return the way we came up is the shortest way back but if time and inclination allow we can head to the north-east to go through Gullet Wood to reach the Shire Ditch below Hangman's Hill and so behind Pink Cottage on the same path described in the previous route. Then instead of the

Level: ♥ ♥
Length: 2 miles (3.25 kms) or 6 miles (9.5 kms) to include Little Malvern.
Ascent: 560 feet (170 metres).
Terrain: Woodland paths and field paths. Some steep inclines, some road walking.
Park and start: Stanway car park (pay and display). GR 766382.
Information: Refreshments at Wynd's Point on A449 (snack bar and hotel).

climb beside British Camp Reservoir turn on the path east and north beyond Underhills Farm to gain Little Malvern hamlet. A walk northwards, first on the A4104 then A449 brings us to Little Malvern Roman Catholic church where we can inspect Sir Edward Elgar's grave in the grounds below the church (see second box detail).

Our return is a direct walk to the south, past Underhills Farm, across Shadybank Common and so to the starting point at Berrow Downs.

1 Park at Stanway car park (pay and display) at Berrow Downs, part of Castlemorton Common. GR 766382.

2 Head west across the slope towards the confines of woodland that herald the ravine called The Gullet. We pass close by the southern bank of the dramatic lake-filled quarry which heralds a steep climb though Gullet Wood to the watershed.

A bewildering meeting of tracks occurs here, not far

The 120 feet (36 metres) high obelisk on that west-facing spur overlooking Eastnor Castle's deer park is a true eye-catcher from miles around. It was the creation of the first Earl Somers (John Somers Cocks) who also had Eastnor Castle built to designs by Robert Smirke. Somers was a Lt Colonel in the Worcestershire Yeomanry Cavalry and fought in the Napoleonic wars. The stone obelisk commemorates Somer's son who fought with Wellington and was killed at Burgos in the Peninsular War.

The structure is not particularly secure these days and as visitors we see pieces of masonry lying around its foot. A fence has been erected to deter close approaches! The spur-top here is ablaze with native wild flowers in summertime.

Quarry pool in The Gullet.

The Somers Obelisk.

south of Peacock Villa. We aim west, on a broad track curving round the south side of the spur ahead. Very soon we come in sight of the giant Somers Obelisk, our first objective.

Turn back the way we have come as far as the junction of tracks.

Peacock Villa above Gullet Wood.

Left: Midsummer Hill from path to the Somers Obelisk.

Little Malvern Court.

5 Either return down The Gullet the way we came up or –

6 Turn left (north) towards Peacock Villa but before reaching it fork right to pass through woodland then come out on the western slopes of Swinyard Hill, close below the top of Hangman's Hill.

7 Turn back to the south-east and take the first path back

Sir Edward Elgar wrote to an old family friend a year before his death "my beloved Teme, surely the loveliest river". He asked to be buried in an unmarked grave at the confluence of the Teme with the Severn, where the lush plain sweeps away from Worcester's edge towards the backdrop of the Malvern Hills. He planned, while ill in 1933, to go picnicking on the banks of the Teme the following summer but it was not to be – he died in February, 1934. For various reasons his request to lie forever beside the Teme was not met and he was laid to rest beside Lady Elgar (who had died in 1920) in the shady graveyard of St. Woolstan's at Little Malvern. The grave is signposted and easy to locate.

to the left and soon pass close behind Pink Cottage (the same route here as described in the previous route).

8 We soon descend across Shadybank Common and head north past Underhills Farm to reach Little Malvern hamlet on the A4104 road.

9 If time and inclination allow go north on the main road, joining the A449 as its drops from Wynd's Point, and soon we come to Littlke Malvern Roman Catholic church on the right (see Sir Edward Elgar's grave in the grounds below the church).

10 Turn back now, again passing Little Malvern Court as we head south on the track/path to cross Shadybank Common en route for the Stanway car park at Berrow Downs.

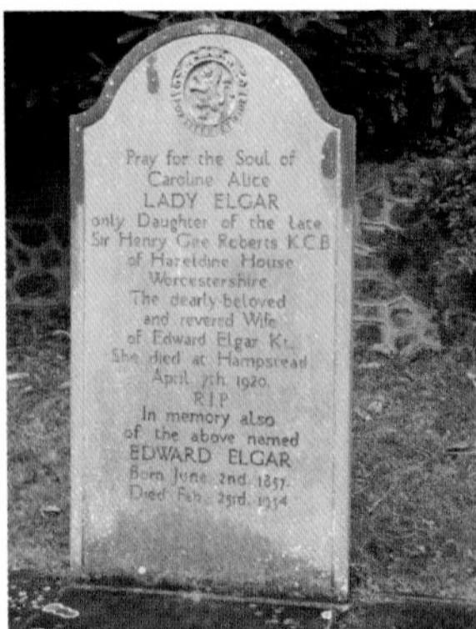

Elgar's Grave at Little Malvern.

9 Colwall to Great Malvern

A linear walk – letting the train take the strain!

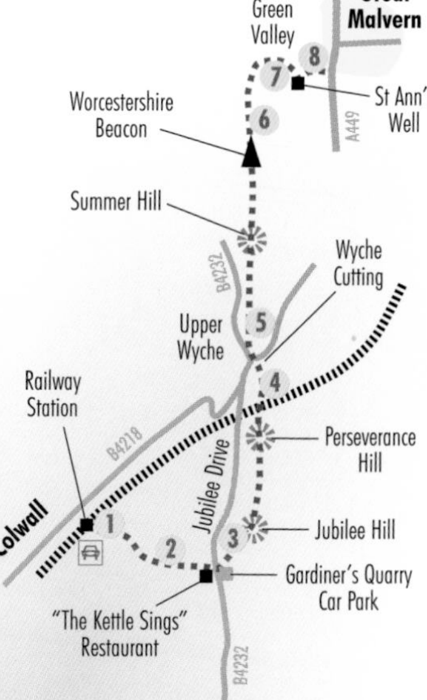

The coming of the Great Western Railway to Great Malvern and on under the Malvern Hills to Hereford in 1861 brought a possibility of living far out in the countryside and commuting to work in places like Worcester, Hereford and beyond. Such possibilities caused the rapid expansion of Colwall, formerly a remote Herefordshire village at the western foot of this hill range.

We, too, can make use of the railway by travelling to Colwall and starting a linear walk north-east over the highest summit to finish at Great Malvern, a distance of some 4 miles (6.5 kms).

Level: ❖ ❖ ❖
Length: 4 miles (6.5 kms).
Ascent: 1,445 feet (440 metres).
Terrain: Field paths, steep hillsides and good paths in the last section.
Start: Colwall railway station. GR 756425.
Information: Great Malvern Tourist Information Centre. Tel. 01684 892289. Trains: Central Trains. Tel. 0121 634 2040. First Great Western. Tel. 0845 7000125. Refreshments in Colwall, "The Kettle Sings" restaurant, and St Ann's Well.

Leaving Colwall railway station we head on a path up the foothill slopes due east and after crossing the first field we fork right up steepening ground to gain the track below Jubilee Drive just north of "The Kettle Sings" restaurant (refreshments, see Walk 6). Heading up the west flank of Jubilee Hill we then turn north along the watershed beside the Shire Ditch, cross the Wyche Cutting and continue the climb to Worcestershire Beacon via Summer Hill.

In fine weather, summer or winter, we have the pleasure of that 360 degrees view across half of England. It is a straightforward descent by St Ann's Well to Great Malvern (see Walk 5).

Herefordshire and the Welsh mountains from Jubilee Drive.

If Sir Edward Elgar is the composer most closely associated with the Malvern Hills then it is the poetry of William Langland we automatically connect with the area. Probably born at Cleobury Mortimer in neighbouring Shropshire about 1332 his vision "concerning Piers the Plowman" sets the scene for the essential experience of England. Langland's "Plowman" gazed down from the Malvern crest and thought he surveyed "all of England".

That impression is as true today as in the fourteenth century – he saw in his dream "as if he had been looking downward to plain and the Severn", to quote the late Geoffrey Grigson writing in 1962.

"A faire felde ful of folke…
Of alle manner of men, the mene and the riche,
Worching and wandryng as the worlde asketh"

1 Start from Colwall railway station. GR 756425.

2 Walk due east across the first field then take the right-hand path that climbs steadily to gain the lane close to "The Kettle Sings" restaurant, just below the line of Jubilee Drive.

3 Head up right to Gardiner's Quarry car park overlooking

The summit of Worcestershire Beacon.

The Severn Valley from Worcestershire Beacon.

Jubilee Drive then head slantwise to the summit of Jubilee Hill.

4 Continue due north along the main watershed, over Perseverance Hill, to descend to the B4218 road close to the Wyche Cutting at Upper Wyche.

5 Just where the B4232 road heads north from the B4218 road take the lane to a public car park which gives access to the path continuing north alongside the Shire Ditch, over Summer Hill and climb to the top of Worcestershire Beacon.

6 Descend north again on one of several good paths leading to the top of Green Valley.

7 Descend right (east) down Green Valley to reach St Ann's Well (refreshments).

The path to Worcestershire Beacon.

Lady Foley lobbied for a railway route that served Malvern then passed in a tunnel beneath the Malvern Hills and went on via Colwall to Hereford.

Work on the tunnel, known locally as "Colwall Tunnel", began in 1856 but soon progress came to a snail's pace as some of the hardest rock on earth was encountered by navvies using only hand tools. It is said that Mammoth bones were excavated close to one tunnel entrance. The two working faces eventually met in July, 1860 and the tunnel opened to traffic a year later.

The brick lining of the tunnel became weakened by the blast from locomotive chimneys so the Great Western Railway decided to construct a larger, single track tunnel alongside the original one. Work began in 1924 and it opened in August, 1926 but two-way working using both tunnels never came into being. An interesting off-shoot from this second tunnel's construction was that spoil from the bore was originally piled near the Malvern Wells (northern) portal and in more recent times was used in constructing local motorways.

Great Malvern Priory and the Abbey Hotel.

8 A good path descends steeply below St Ann's Well to the centre of Great Malvern and journey's end.

St Ann's Well.

10 On foot to Chase End Hill

Exploring the southernmost limit of the Malvern Hills.

The main road linking Tewkesbury, at the confluence of Avon with Severn, and Ledbury (A438) cuts through the Malvern Hills at the scattered settlement of Hollybush. To the south of this highway the hill range throws up its very last tops. These are Ragged Stone Hill, 833 feet (254 metres) and Chase End Hill, 626 feet (191 metres) and an attractive circular route makes a fitting end to this wonderful upland terrain.

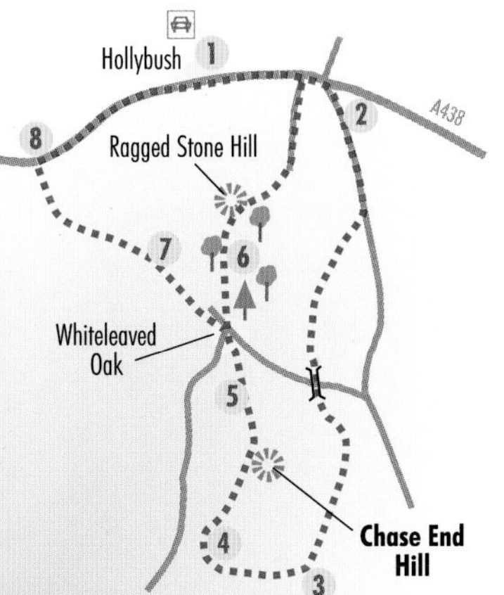

A good part of both Ragged Stone Hill and Chase End Hill is now Access Land where we are free to wander at will off official footpaths so this allows us to reach the actual modest tops of this last gasp of the backbone that first reared heavenwards far away overlooking North Malvern.

Level:
Length: 3.5 miles (5.5 kms) or 3.75 miles (6 kms).
Ascent: 720 feet (220 metres) or 425 feet (130 metres).
Terrain: Field paths, lanes and steep hillsides.
Park and start: Car park at western edge of Hollybush. GR 758369.
Information: Refreshments at inns at Welland, Rye Steet and Ledbury.

A pretty, modest route can be commenced at Hollybush, in the gap in the hills just south of Midsummer Hill. We wander through the hidden, secret country around Whiteleaved Oak, climb Chase End Hill and return either over or upon the western flank of Ragged Stone Hill. A fairly gentle ending to our explorations of the magnificent Malverns.

1 Start from the car park at the western edge of Hollybush. GR 758369. Then walk east along the A438 to the first cross-roads.

2 Turn south (right) along the narrow lane for about a quarter of a mile (1.5 kms) then fork off right along the original drive to Bromesberrow Place.

3 The drive crosses a public lane on a bridge but we continue on the old driveway a further half mile (.8 km) to turn west (right) on a path through woodland before

Summer afternoon on Castlemorton Common.

Lambert's Cottage, Whiteleaved Oak.

The Malvern Hills Conservators is a public body established in 1884 to maintain the land as close to nature as possible, to secure open spaces and to protect the rights of registered commoners. The area they protect is the remnant of the original medieval Chase that stretched to the western bank of the River Severn.

The different habitats of the Hills and the adjacent Commons were the result of centuries of grazing but this has slowly decreased over decades so that bracken and scrubland has spread. Sheep and beef cattle have been re-introduced to control this spread of scrub and trees.

It is said that a million visitors tramp the Malvern Hills annually. The various Acts of Parliament give access to pedestrians and horse riders and, more so these days, cyclists. Full time wardens supported by volunteers patrol the entire area to enforce byelaws and to answer visitors' enquiries. Further information: Malvern Hills Conservators, Manor House, Grange Road, Malvern, Worcestershire, WR14 3EY. Tel. 01684 892002. www.malvernhills.org.uk

crossing the open, southern slopes of Chase End Hill.

4 Keep right to swing up to the north to the trig. pillar on the summit of Chase End Hill. We now stand at 626 feet (191 metres) to look out over the sprawling lowland and maybe hear traffic on the M50 motorway to the south.

Thistles below Midsummer Hill at Hollybush.

Cottage at Hollybush below Ragged Stone Hill.

Hillside Cottage at Whiteleaved Oak below Chase End Hill.

5 Head down to the footpath as it goes north the short distance to the lane in the middle of Whiteleaved Oak.

6 Continue a short step north from the bend in the lane and either turn up right, through the trees, to continue up to the 833 feet (254 metres) top of Ragged Stone Hill then drop down north-east to the lane that goes along to join the A438 in Hollybush. Now turn left along it to our starting point; or –

7 Go back from the summit the way we climbed up. When we regain the edge of the hamlet turn right (north-west) along the path that leads to the A438 near Fowlet Farm.

8 Turn right along the A438 to our starting point.

The Malvern Hills from Castlemorton Common.